It's Mine!

By Janine Amos   Illustrated by Annabel Spenceley
Consultant Rachael Underwood

Gareth Stevens Publishing
A WORLD ALMANAC EDUCATION GROUP COMPANY

Please visit our web site at: www.garethstevens.com
For a free color catalog describing Gareth Stevens Publishing's
list of high-quality books and multimedia programs, call
1-800-542-2595 (USA) or 1-800-387-3178 (Canada).
Gareth Stevens Publishing's fax: (414) 332-3567.

Library of Congress Cataloging-in-Publication Data

Amos, Janine.
    It's mine! / by Janine Amos; illustrated by Annabel Spenceley.
      p. cm. — (Courteous kids)
    Includes bibliographical references.
    Summary: Two brief stories demonstrate the importance of sharing, being careful
with the property of others, and taking turns.
    ISBN 0-8368-3609-X (lib. bdg.)
    1. Social interaction in children—Juvenile literature. 2. Problem solving in children—
Juvenile literature. [1. Sharing. 2. Behavior. 3. Etiquette. 4. Conduct of life.]
    I. Spenceley, Annabel, ill. II. Title.
    BF723.S62A47   2003
    177'.1—dc21   2002036479

This edition first published in 2003 by
Gareth Stevens Publishing
A World Almanac Education Group Company
330 West Olive Street, Suite 100
Milwaukee, Wisconsin 53212 USA

Series editor: Dorothy L. Gibbs
Graphic designer: Katherine A. Goedheer
Cover design: Joel Bucaro

This edition © 2003 by Gareth Stevens, Inc. First published by Cherrytree Press,
a subsidiary of Evans Brothers Limited. © 1999 by Cherrytree (a member of the
Evans Group of Publishers), 2A Portman Mansions, Chiltern Street, London
W1U 6NR, United Kingdom. This U.S. edition published under license from
Evans Brothers Limited. Additional end matter © 2003 by Gareth Stevens, Inc.

All rights reserved. No part of this book may be reproduced, stored in a retrieval
system, or transmitted in any form or by any means, electronic, mechanical,
photocopying, recording, or otherwise, without the prior written permission
of the copyright holder.

Printed in the United States of America

1 2 3 4 5 6 7 8 9 07 06 05 04 03

Note to Parents and Teachers

The questions that appear in **boldface** type can be used to initiate
discussion with your children or class. Encourage them to think of
possible answers before continuing with the story.

The Treasure Map

Everyone is making treasure maps on gold paper.
There is only one piece of gold paper left.

"It's mine!" says Amy. "I want it!" says Emma.
What do you think they could do?

5

"We can both use it!" Amy tells Emma.
Amy starts working at one end of the paper.

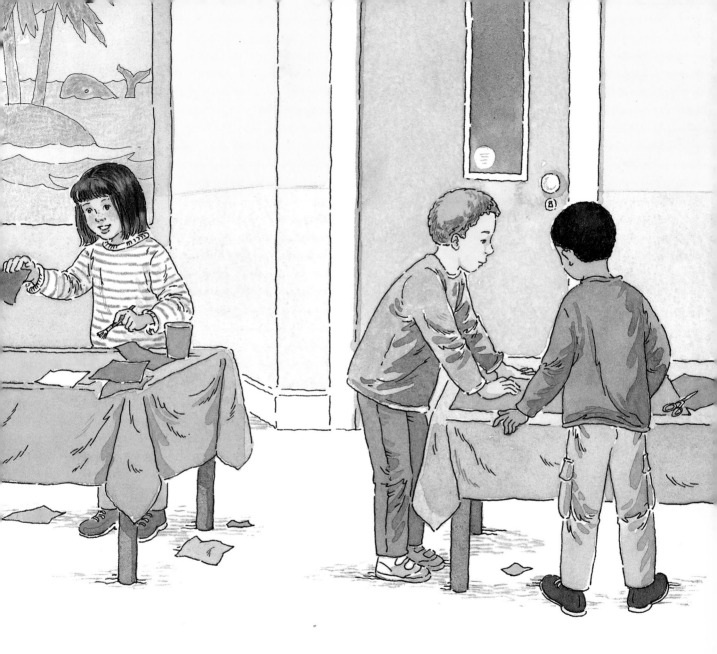

Emma agrees and starts working
at the other end of the paper.

Amy and Emma make a treasure map together.

It looks great, thinks Emma.

9

"The treasure map is finished!" says Amy.
"I'll put it on my bedroom wall."

"I want it on my bedroom wall!" says Emma.
How do you think Emma feels?

11

"I've got an idea," Steve tells them.

"One of you can take the treasure map home today.
The other one can take it home tomorrow."

"Yes, let's take turns!" says Amy.

"Who will go first?" asks Emma.
"You can!" Amy offers.

"Thanks, Amy," says Emma.
"Tomorrow, it will be your turn!"

16

The Tiger Mask

Amal has come to play at Colin's house.

Colin has made a mask. It is a tiger mask.

Colin puts on the mask. "Grrr!" he says.

20

Colin creeps toward Amal.
"Grrr! Grrr!" he growls.

21

Amal grabs the tiger mask.
"I want it!" he says.

Colin pulls away.
"It's mine!" he shouts.

Amal pulls on the mask.
Colin pulls away.

24

Then, the mask breaks.
How do you think Colin feels?

Colin starts to cry.

Colin's mother comes over.
"Oh, dear," she says, "the mask is broken."
What do you think they could do?

27

"We can fix it," says Amal.
"We can tape it back together."

Colin gets the tape, and
Amal helps Colin fix the mask.

29

Now Colin is a tiger again.

And Amal is Batman.

Saying "It's mine!" lets someone else know that you both want the same thing, often at the same time. You might even feel that what you want belongs to you. Try to work out the problem by talking it over, then sharing, taking turns, or finding something else to play with.

More Books to Read

Friends. Kim Lewis (Candlewick Press)

I Want It. Elizabeth Crary (Parenting Press)

My Friend and I. Lisa Jahn-Clough
(Houghton Mifflin)

J177.1
Amos   Amos, Janine
                 It's Mine

MARTIN LUTHER KING, JR.